Table of Contents

Introduction

Welcome to "The Ultimate Guide on How to Start a Yoga Instruction Business." I'm thrilled you're here and interested in diving into the wonderful world of yoga instruction. This guide is crafted specifically for entrepreneurs like you who are eager to blend their passion for yoga with a successful business venture. Whether you're driven by a love for yoga or a desire to help others enhance their physical and mental well-being, this book has got you covered with all the knowledge and strategies you'll need to get started.

Yoga instruction is truly transformative. It's not just about teaching poses; it's about fostering overall health and wellness. Through a blend of physical postures, breathing exercises, meditation, and mindfulness, yoga creates a holistic practice that benefits people of all ages and fitness levels. As a yoga instructor, you'll have the incredible opportunity to positively impact people's lives, helping them find balance, relaxation, and personal growth.

Starting a yoga instruction business is more than just a career move—it's a way to live your passion every day. Imagine the freedom to design your own schedule, do what you love, and make a significant difference in others' lives. Plus, with the increasing popularity of yoga, there's a growing market ready for dedicated and skilled instructors like you.

This guide is your roadmap to success. It's divided into ten comprehensive chapters, each focusing on a crucial aspect of launching and running a thriving yoga instruction business. We'll start with the basics, introducing you to the concept of yoga instruction, its myriad benefits, and the structure and purpose of this guide. From there, we'll dive into assessing your skills and qualifications, understanding your target market, and developing a solid business plan.

We'll also cover the nitty-gritty details like legal and regulatory considerations, setting up your business operations, and building a brand and online presence that stands out. You'll learn how to attract clients, network effectively, and deliver exceptional service to your students. And as your business grows, we'll explore strategies to help you expand and stay connected with your community.

Throughout this guide, you'll find practical tips, valuable insights from seasoned yoga instructors, and real-life examples that will inspire and guide you on your entrepreneurial journey. So, are you ready to dive into the exciting world of starting a yoga instruction business? Let's embark on this fulfilling adventure together. Your journey starts now!

Chapter 1: Introduction to Yoga Instruction

Welcome to the world of yoga instruction! This chapter is all about introducing you to the wonderful art and practice of teaching yoga. Yoga is an ancient discipline that goes beyond mere physical exercise; it encompasses guiding individuals through various poses, breathing exercises, and meditation techniques to promote physical, mental, and spiritual well-being.

Yoga has gained immense popularity worldwide, and it's no wonder why. The benefits of yoga are numerous, and its positive impact on overall health is well-documented. As a yoga instructor, you play a crucial role in promoting physical and mental well-being among your students. Through your guidance, individuals can develop strength, flexibility, and balance in their bodies. Regular yoga practice can improve posture, increase stamina, and enhance overall fitness levels.

But yoga is not just about physical fitness. It also nurtures mental and emotional well-being. Through breath control and meditation, yoga helps individuals reduce stress and anxiety, improve mental clarity, and find inner peace. This holistic approach to wellness is what makes yoga so special and transformative.

Starting a yoga instruction business presents numerous advantages. First and foremost, it allows you to share your passion for yoga with others and make a positive impact on their lives. As a yoga instructor, you have the opportunity to inspire and guide individuals on their transformational journey towards physical and mental wellness. There is something incredibly fulfilling about watching your students grow and flourish through their yoga practice.

Additionally, starting a yoga instruction business provides the flexibility to work on your own terms. You can choose your own schedule, set your rates, and determine the types of classes you want to offer. This level of autonomy allows you to pursue your passion while creating a fulfilling career. Whether you prefer teaching in a studio, offering private sessions, or conducting online classes, the possibilities are endless.

The purpose of this guide is to provide you with a comprehensive roadmap on how to start a successful yoga instruction business. Each chapter will discuss essential aspects of establishing and growing your business, providing practical tips and strategies to ensure your success. From setting up your business and marketing your services to creating a positive client experience and managing your finances, we've got you covered.

So, let's delve into the chapters that will guide you through the process of starting and running a yoga instruction business. Whether you're a seasoned yoga practitioner looking to turn your passion into a profession or someone new to the world of yoga, this guide will provide you with the knowledge and tools you need to succeed.

Welcome to the beginning of your journey as a yoga instructor. Let's embark on this path together and create a business that not only thrives but also brings joy, health, and well-being to others. Namaste.

Chapter 2: Assessing Your Skills and Qualifications

Before you dive into starting your own yoga instruction business, it's crucial to take a step back and really evaluate your skills and qualifications. This self-assessment isn't just a formality—it's a way to understand your strengths, areas where you excel, and the specific types of yoga classes you are truly qualified to teach. By taking the time to do this, you can position yourself more effectively in the market and better cater to your target audience.

Evaluating Your Background, Training, and Experience

First things first, let's reflect on your journey in yoga. Here are some questions to guide you:

1. How long have you been practicing yoga?

Think about your personal journey as a yoga practitioner. How many years have you been dedicated to the practice? Your years of experience form the backbone of your teaching skills, giving you a strong foundation to build on.

2. Have you completed any formal yoga teacher training programs?

Make a list of any certifications you've obtained, including the duration of these training programs. These credentials are more than just pieces of paper—they're badges of credibility that can set you apart as an instructor.

3. Have you attended workshops or specialized training in specific yoga styles or techniques?

Detail any additional training you've undergone. Whether it's workshops, retreats, or specialized courses, this extra training enhances your knowledge and skills, making you a more well-rounded instructor.

4. Have you taught yoga classes before?

Reflect on your teaching experience, whether it's one-on-one sessions or group classes. Think about the size of the classes you've taught and the feedback you've received. Teaching experience is invaluable as it demonstrates your ability to lead and guide students effectively.

Identifying Your Strengths and Areas of Expertise

Next, let's hone in on your strengths and areas of expertise within yoga instruction:

1. What are your personal strengths as a yoga practitioner and instructor?

Consider what makes you unique. Is it your teaching style, your ability to communicate effectively, or perhaps your talent for creating a welcoming and inclusive environment? Highlighting these strengths will contribute to your success as a yoga instructor.

2. Do you have expertise in specific yoga styles?

Identify any particular yoga styles you're well-versed in, like Hatha, Vinyasa, Ashtanga, or Yin yoga. Specializing in certain styles can help you attract a specific target market that's looking for exactly what you offer.

3. Are you knowledgeable in teaching yoga to special populations?

If you have experience working with seniors, pregnant women, individuals with injuries, or specific communities, make sure to note this. Your expertise in these areas can set you apart from other instructors and help you attract a niche audience.

Determining the Types of Yoga Classes You Are Qualified to Teach

Now, let's figure out the types of yoga classes you're qualified to teach:

1. What is your level of expertise in different class formats?

Reflect on your comfort level with teaching beginner, intermediate, or advanced yoga classes. Consider your confidence in leading students through various sequences and poses, ensuring that you can cater to a range of skill levels.

2. Can you teach specialized classes, such as prenatal yoga, restorative yoga, or yoga for athletes?

Evaluate your qualifications and experience in teaching these specialized classes. These classes often cater to specific populations or address particular needs, which can be a significant draw for your business.

By conducting this comprehensive assessment of your skills and qualifications, you gain a deeper understanding of your strengths and areas of expertise. This understanding allows you to position yourself effectively in the market and tailor your services to meet the needs of your target audience. Take the time to reflect on your yoga journey and teaching experience. Embrace the unique qualities that make you a capable and skilled yoga instructor, ready to inspire and lead your future students.

Chapter 3: Understanding Your Target Market

When it comes to launching and growing your yoga instruction business, understanding your target market is absolutely essential. It's not just about knowing who might be interested in yoga, but really getting into the specifics of what different groups need, want, and expect from their yoga practice. By defining your target market segments, conducting thorough market research, and finding ways to differentiate and specialize your services, you'll be better equipped to tailor your offerings to meet the unique needs and preferences of your audience.

Defining Your Target Market Segments

To effectively connect with your audience, it's important to break down your market into specific segments. Here are some key segments you might consider:

- **Beginners**: These are individuals who are new to yoga. They might be looking for introductory classes that cover basic poses and breathing techniques. This segment often needs more guidance and support to get started on their yoga journey.
- **Seniors**: Older adults may have specific physical limitations or health concerns.

Offering gentle or chair yoga classes tailored to their needs can make yoga more accessible and beneficial for them. This segment appreciates a focus on safety and modifications.

- **Pregnant Women**: Pregnancy yoga classes are designed to support the physical and emotional well-being of expectant mothers. This segment requires specialized knowledge to ensure the safety and comfort of both the mother and baby. Classes often include modifications and techniques to help with common pregnancy-related issues.
- **Specific Communities**: Your target market might also include people from particular communities, such as athletes, corporate professionals, or individuals seeking stress relief. Each of these groups has unique needs and preferences that you can address with specialized classes or programs.

Conducting Market Research

Market research is your tool for understanding the needs, preferences, and fitness goals of your target audience. Here are some effective ways to conduct this research:

- **Surveys**: Create online surveys or questionnaires to gather detailed information about your audience's preferences, goals, and challenges related to yoga. This can give you a broad overview of what different segments are looking for.

- **Interviews**: Conduct one-on-one interviews with members of your target market. These conversations can provide deeper insights into their motivations, preferences, and expectations, helping you to refine your offerings even further.
- **Competitive Analysis**: Take a close look at your competitors. What services do they offer? Who are they targeting? Are there gaps in the market that you could fill? Understanding the competitive landscape can help you position your business more effectively.
- **Online Research**: Utilize online platforms like social media groups, forums, and industry websites to gather additional information and insights. These platforms can be a goldmine for understanding current trends and what your target market is talking about.

Identifying Opportunities for Differentiation and Specialization

With your market segments defined and your research in hand, the next step is to identify opportunities for differentiation and specialization. This is where you can really set yourself apart from the competition and cater to specific niche needs within your market. Here are some strategies:

- **Differentiate Based on Yoga Style**: If you have expertise in a particular yoga style, such as Hatha, Vinyasa, or Ashtanga, you can position yourself as a specialist in that area. This can attract students who are specifically interested in that style.

- **Specialize in Specific Populations**: If you have experience teaching yoga to seniors, pregnant women, or individuals with specific health conditions, consider offering specialized classes tailored to these groups. Your expertise in these areas can become a significant draw for clients looking for customized yoga experiences.
- **Offer Unique Classes or Workshops**: Think creatively about how you can offer something different. This might include unique class formats or workshops that address particular needs or interests within your target market. For example, you could offer a workshop on yoga for stress relief, yoga for athletes, or mindfulness and meditation techniques.

By understanding your target market, conducting thorough market research, and identifying opportunities for differentiation and specialization, you can position your yoga instruction business for success. Tailoring your offerings to meet the specific needs of your target audience will not only attract more clients but also build a loyal customer base that values the personalized experience you provide. Remember, the key to success in the yoga business is not just about teaching yoga, but about creating meaningful connections and experiences that resonate with your students.

Chapter 4: Developing Your Business Plan

Hey there, aspiring yoga entrepreneur! If you're gearing up to launch a successful yoga instruction business, developing a comprehensive business plan is a crucial step. Think of it as your roadmap, guiding you through important decisions about your goals, services, pricing, and marketing strategy. Let's dive into the key components of creating a solid business plan.

Outline Your Business Goals, Mission Statement, and Core Values

First things first, let's talk about outlining your business goals, mission statement, and core values. This foundational step will help you define the purpose and vision of your business, giving you a clear framework for your decision-making process.

Start by considering what you hope to achieve through your yoga instruction business. Are you aiming to create a welcoming community for yoga practitioners? Do you want to help individuals enhance their physical and mental well-being? Clearly defining your business goals will provide direction and keep you focused on your mission.

Next, it's time to craft a compelling mission statement that captures the essence of your business. Your mission statement should succinctly describe the purpose of your business and convey the value you intend to provide to your clients. For instance, "Our mission is to create a nurturing space where individuals can explore their yoga practice and cultivate a deeper connection with their mind, body, and spirit."

Equally important are your core values. These values will guide your decision-making process and shape the culture of your business. Think about what's important to you—maybe it's inclusivity, integrity, or continuous growth. By identifying and clearly articulating your core values, you can attract like-minded individuals who resonate with your business philosophy.

Define Your Yoga Services, Pricing Structure, and Revenue Projections

Now, let's move on to defining your yoga services, pricing structure, and revenue projections. This is where you'll outline what you offer and how you'll make money.

Start by considering the types of classes you'll offer and the level of expertise you'll bring to each session. Will you focus on specific yoga styles or cater to special populations? This can help differentiate your business and attract your target market.

When it comes to setting your pricing structure, market research is key. Look at the prices of other yoga instruction businesses in your area. Consider the value you're providing to your clients, your level of expertise, and any additional services or perks you might offer. Make sure your pricing is competitive and aligns with the target market you're catering to.

In addition to pricing, it's crucial to estimate your revenue projections. Think about factors such as the number of classes you plan to offer, the average class size, and the number of clients you expect to attract. This will give you a realistic idea of your income potential and help you set financial goals for your business.

Create a Marketing Strategy to Reach and Attract Your Target Market

A strong marketing strategy is vital for the success of your yoga instruction business. It will help you raise awareness about your services, attract potential clients, and build a loyal customer base.

Begin by identifying your target market and understanding their needs, preferences, and fitness goals. This will help you tailor your marketing messages and reach the right audience. For example, if your target market includes beginners, focus on highlighting the benefits of starting a yoga practice and creating a welcoming environment for newcomers.

Utilize a mix of online and offline marketing channels to promote your business. Consider creating a professional website that showcases your classes, schedule, and instructor credentials. Social media platforms are also powerful tools for sharing content, engaging with your audience, and promoting special offers or events.

Don't forget about the power of local partnerships. Collaborate with local businesses and organizations to expand your reach. This could involve offering free yoga workshops or demonstrations at wellness centers, teaming up with other fitness professionals, or participating in community events. Networking and building relationships with yoga studios, gyms, and wellness centers can also lead to referrals and partnerships.

Putting It All Together

Developing a business plan that outlines your goals, mission statement, core values, and marketing strategy will provide a strong foundation for your yoga instruction business. By defining your services, pricing structure, and revenue projections, you can effectively position yourself in the market and attract your target audience.

With a solid business plan in place, you'll be well-equipped to navigate the challenges and opportunities that come with starting your own yoga instruction business. So, take a deep breath, stay focused, and get ready to embark on this exciting journey. You've got this!

Chapter 5: Legal and Regulatory Considerations

Starting a yoga instruction business is an exciting venture, but it requires careful attention to legal and regulatory considerations to ensure everything runs smoothly. This chapter will guide you through the essential legal aspects of starting a yoga instruction business, helping you operate in a legal and professional manner.

Understanding the Legal Requirements

Before opening your yoga instruction business, it's crucial to understand the legal requirements involved. This includes obtaining the necessary certifications, permits, and licenses.

Certifications: Many yoga studios and fitness centers require instructors to hold a Yoga Alliance certification. This certification demonstrates that you have completed a recognized yoga teacher training program and have met the required standards of instruction. Research the specific certification requirements in your area and ensure that you have the necessary credentials. Having a recognized certification not only boosts your credibility but also assures your clients that you are well-trained and qualified.

Permits and Licenses: Check with your local government or municipality to determine if any permits or licenses are required to operate a yoga instruction business. This may include a general business license or specific permits for operating a fitness facility. Failing to obtain the necessary permits can result in fines or legal consequences. It's always better to be proactive and ensure all your paperwork is in order before you start offering classes.

Complying with Regulations

In addition to obtaining the necessary certifications and permits, it's essential to comply with the regulations governing fitness instruction services. These regulations are designed to protect both the instructor and the clients.

Fitness Instruction Services: Familiarize yourself with the regulations that govern fitness instruction services in your area. This includes maintaining a safe and clean environment, adhering to health and safety standards, and following any specific guidelines for operating a fitness facility. Understanding these regulations will help you create a safe and welcoming space for your clients.

Client Confidentiality: As a yoga instructor, you will often come into contact with personal information shared by your clients. It's crucial to respect and protect their privacy by upholding client confidentiality. This means not discussing or sharing any personal information shared during class or private sessions without the explicit permission of the client. Trust is a key component of the instructor-client relationship, and maintaining confidentiality is vital to building that trust.

Safety Standards: Prioritize the safety of your clients by following established safety standards. This includes maintaining proper equipment, ensuring a clean and hazard-free environment, and having emergency procedures in place. Regularly inspect and maintain your yoga space and equipment to ensure they are in good working condition. A safe environment encourages clients to return and recommend your classes to others.

Considering Liability Insurance

Liability insurance is an important consideration for any yoga instructor. It provides financial protection in case a client is injured or property damage occurs during a yoga class or session. While yoga is generally a low-risk activity, accidents can happen, and liability insurance can help protect your business and clients.

Research Insurance Providers: Look for insurance providers that offer liability coverage for yoga instructors. Compare different policies and coverage options to find the one that best suits your needs and budget. Having liability insurance will give you peace of mind and protect your business assets in case of unexpected accidents or claims.

By understanding the legal requirements, complying with regulations, and considering liability insurance, you can operate your yoga instruction business with confidence and professionalism.

Ensuring that you are legally compliant will help you establish a strong foundation for your business and protect both yourself and your clients. Remember, a well-regulated and insured business is not only a legal necessity but also a mark of professionalism that can set you apart in the competitive world of yoga instruction.

Chapter 6: Setting Up Your Business Operations

Hey there, future yoga mogul! Let's talk about one of the most crucial steps in launching your yoga instruction business: setting up your business operations. This process involves a few key components, including choosing the right business structure, registering your business, setting up your yoga space and equipment, and developing policies and procedures for smooth operations. Let's break it down together.

Choose a Business Structure and Register Your Business

Before you officially kick off your yoga instruction business, you need to choose the right business structure and get your business registered with the appropriate authorities. The most common business structures you can consider are sole proprietorship, partnership, limited liability company (LLC), and corporation. Each of these structures has its own set of advantages and considerations, so take some time to research and pick the one that aligns with your goals and offers the legal and financial protections you need.

Once you've settled on a business structure, you'll need to register your business name and secure any required licenses or permits. Don't forget to apply for necessary tax identifications, like an Employer Identification Number (EIN) or a state tax identification number. Registering your business is essential not only for legal compliance but also to enable you to open a business bank account and establish your financials.

Set Up Your Yoga Space, Equipment, and Scheduling Systems

Creating an inviting and conducive environment for your yoga classes is essential. Start by choosing a suitable location that offers enough space to accommodate your students comfortably. Whether you're renting a studio, converting a room in your home, or offering outdoor classes, make sure the space aligns with your target market and includes the necessary amenities and ventilation.

Next, invest in quality yoga equipment. You'll need yoga mats, blocks, straps, bolsters, and blankets to provide your students with the support and comfort they need during practice. Consider the diverse needs of your students, including those with injuries or special conditions, and have appropriate props available to assist them.

A reliable scheduling system is also crucial. This system should allow students to easily book classes and manage their attendance. You can set this up through a website, booking software, or even a simple spreadsheet. Ensure that your scheduling system is user-friendly, accessible, and provides clear information about class times, locations, and any prerequisites or requirements.

Develop Policies and Procedures for Client Registration, Waivers, and Class Management

Having clear policies and procedures in place for client registration, waivers, and class management is essential for running a professional and organized business. Develop a streamlined process for new students to register, providing their contact information, health history, and necessary waivers.

Make sure you obtain proper liability waivers from your students, acknowledging their understanding of the risks involved in practicing yoga. These waivers should clearly outline the terms and conditions of participation, as well as any health or safety guidelines.

Establish guidelines for class management, including attendance policies, cancellation and refund policies, and any specific rules or requirements for your classes. Clearly communicate these policies to your students, either through your website, welcome emails, or a printed student handbook.

Putting It All Together

By setting up your business operations effectively, you'll be able to create a professional and efficient yoga instruction business. Choosing the right business structure, registering your business, setting up your space and equipment, and developing clear policies and procedures will lay a solid foundation for your success.

So, take a deep breath, roll out your mat, and get ready to embark on this exciting journey. With these steps in place, you'll be well-equipped to navigate the challenges and opportunities that come with starting your own yoga instruction business. Namaste!

Chapter 7: Building Your Brand and Online Presence

In today's digital age, having a strong brand and online presence for your yoga instruction business is essential. Your brand identity should reflect your yoga philosophy, teaching style, and values, helping you attract the right audience and stand out from competitors. Additionally, a professional website and effective use of social media and online marketing strategies will raise awareness about your business and attract potential clients. Let's dive into how you can build a compelling brand and a robust online presence for your yoga instruction business.

Developing a Strong Brand Identity

Your brand identity is more than just a logo or a color palette; it's the overall perception and image of your yoga instruction business. Here are some steps to help you develop a strong brand identity:

1. **Define Your Yoga Philosophy**: Reflect on your personal beliefs and values as a yoga practitioner and instructor. What makes your approach to yoga unique? How do you want to connect with your students? Think about the core principles that guide your practice and teaching.

2. **Clarify Your Teaching Style**: Determine the particular teaching style or styles that resonate with you the most. Whether it's vinyasa flow, hatha, yin, or any other style, make sure it aligns with your own practice and interests. Your teaching style should be a natural extension of your yoga philosophy.

3. **Determine Your Target Audience**: Identify the specific demographic or population you want to serve. This could be beginners, seniors, pregnant women, athletes, or any other group you feel passionate about helping. Understanding your target audience will help tailor your classes and marketing efforts to meet their needs.

4. **Create a Consistent Visual Identity**: Develop a logo, color scheme, and typography that represent your brand. These elements should be consistent across all your marketing materials, website, and social media platforms. A cohesive visual identity helps build recognition and trust.

5. **Craft Your Brand Messaging**: Clearly communicate your value proposition and what sets you apart from other yoga instructors. Use your website, social media, and any other promotional materials to convey your unique selling points. Your messaging should resonate with your target audience and reflect your brand's personality.

Creating a Professional Website

A professional website is crucial for establishing credibility and showcasing your yoga instruction services. Here are some tips for creating an effective website:

1. **Keep It User-Friendly**: Ensure that your website is easy to navigate and provides a seamless experience for visitors. Include clear sections for classes, schedules, instructor bios, and contact information. A well-organized website will make it easy for potential clients to find what they need.

2. **Showcase Your Expertise**: Highlight your certifications, training, and experience as a yoga instructor. Share your teaching philosophy and any testimonials from happy students. Demonstrating your expertise will build trust and credibility with potential clients.

3. **Provide Class Information**: Include detailed information about your classes, such as the style, level of difficulty, and duration. Mention any specializations or variations you offer, such as prenatal yoga or yoga for athletes. Clear and comprehensive class descriptions help potential clients choose the right class for their needs.

4. **Share Your Schedule**: Display your class schedule on your website so potential clients can easily see when and where you teach. Consider using an online scheduling tool to make it convenient for students to book classes. An up-to-date schedule helps

clients plan their attendance and reduces the barrier to joining your classes.

5. **Offer Valuable Content**: Create a blog or resources section on your website where you can share informative articles, videos, or guided meditation recordings. This will position you as an industry expert and attract visitors to your site. Valuable content can also improve your website's search engine ranking, making it easier for people to find you online.

Utilizing Social Media and Online Marketing

Social media and online marketing are powerful tools for raising awareness about your yoga instruction business and attracting potential clients. Here are some strategies to consider:

1. **Choose the Right Platforms**: Identify the social media platforms where your target audience is most active. This could be Facebook, Instagram, Twitter, or others. Focus your efforts on these platforms to maximize your reach. Each platform has its strengths, so tailor your content to fit the medium.

2. **Create Engaging Content**: Post regularly and share valuable content that aligns with your brand and resonates with your audience. This could include yoga tips, inspirational quotes, instructional videos, or success stories from your students. Engaging content keeps your audience

interested and encourages them to interact with your posts.

3. **Engage with Your Audience**: Respond to comments and messages promptly, and engage in conversations with your followers. Building relationships and providing personal interaction will help foster a sense of community and loyalty. Active engagement shows that you value your audience and are accessible.

4. **Collaborate with Influencers**: Identify influential individuals or organizations within the yoga community and collaborate with them. This could involve guest blog posts, joint workshops or events, or social media partnerships. Collaborations can expand your reach and introduce your brand to new audiences.

5. **Utilize Online Advertising**: Consider investing in online advertising to increase your reach and target specific audiences. Platforms like Facebook and Google Ads allow you to reach people who may be interested in yoga in your local area. Well-targeted ads can drive traffic to your website and convert visitors into clients.

By developing a strong brand identity, creating a professional website, and utilizing social media and online marketing strategies, you can build a strong online presence and attract clients to your yoga instruction business. Remember to stay consistent with your messaging and keep engaging with your audience to foster lasting relationships. With a well-established online presence, you'll be well on your way to creating a thriving yoga instruction business that resonates with your audience and stands out in the competitive market.

Chapter 8: Acquiring Clients and Networking

Growing your yoga instruction business isn't just about perfecting your poses or deepening your knowledge of the practice; it's also about acquiring clients and building a solid network within the yoga community. In this chapter, we'll delve into effective strategies for reaching potential clients through diverse marketing channels, forming partnerships with yoga studios and wellness centers, and attracting leads by offering free workshops or consultations.

Developing a Marketing Plan

A well-thought-out marketing plan is the backbone of any successful business. For your yoga instruction business, consider the following strategies to attract and retain clients:

Local Advertising: Start by making use of local advertising platforms. Think about placing ads in newspapers, magazines, on the radio, or even on local TV channels. Fitness and wellness publications, community newsletters, and local event websites are also great places to advertise. These channels can help you reach a broader audience within your community.

Online Presence: In today's digital age, having a professional online presence is crucial. Create a sleek, user-friendly website and make sure it's optimized for search engines. Use SEO techniques like keyword research and content optimization to ensure your site ranks higher in search results. Additionally, being active on social media platforms such as Facebook, Instagram, and YouTube can help you connect with potential clients and showcase your offerings.

Community Events: Participating in local community events, health fairs, or wellness expos can be incredibly beneficial. These events are perfect for connecting with individuals who have an interest in fitness and holistic well-being. Setting up a booth can allow you to promote your services and offer special discounts or incentives to attract new clients.

Referrals: Word-of-mouth is powerful. Encourage your existing clients to recommend your classes to their friends, family, and colleagues. To sweeten the deal, consider offering referral incentives like a discounted class or a small gift. This not only motivates your clients to spread the word but also helps you build a loyal customer base.

Networking with Yoga Studios and Wellness Centers

Building strong partnerships with yoga studios, wellness centers, and other complementary businesses can significantly enhance your reach and credibility. Here are some networking strategies to consider:

Reach Out to Local Yoga Studios: Introduce yourself to nearby yoga studios and express your interest in collaboration. Opportunities for guest teaching, workshops, or retreats could be available. Forming relationships with studio owners and instructors can lead to referrals and attract new clients.

Offer Specialty Classes: Collaborate with yoga studios to offer specialty classes that align with their clientele's interests. For instance, if a studio focuses on prenatal yoga, propose a prenatal yoga class series or workshop. This allows you to tap into their existing client base while offering a unique and valuable service.

Partner with Wellness Centers: Explore partnerships with wellness centers, holistic health clinics, or fitness facilities that provide complementary services like massage therapy, chiropractic care, or nutrition counseling. Joint promotions or package deals can attract clients from various wellness modalities, expanding your reach.

Offering Free Workshops or Consultations

Hosting free workshops, introductory classes, or consultations is a fantastic way to showcase your expertise, teaching style, and the value you bring to potential clients. Here's how you can implement these strategies:

Free Workshops: Organize workshops on specific yoga-related topics such as stress management, mindfulness, or yoga for beginners. These sessions can be educational and engaging, allowing potential clients to experience your teaching style firsthand.

Introductory Classes: Offer discounted or free introductory classes for new students interested in trying yoga for the first time. Create a welcoming environment and provide personalized attention to ensure their initial experience is positive and memorable.

Consultations: Provide free consultations for individuals considering starting a regular yoga practice or those with specific health concerns. During these sessions, assess their needs, answer questions, and offer personalized recommendations to help them achieve their unique goals.

By crafting a comprehensive marketing plan, networking with yoga studios and wellness centers, and offering free workshops or consultations, you can effectively attract clients and establish a strong presence in the yoga community. These strategies will help you build a loyal client base and increase your visibility as a yoga instructor.

Chapter 9: Providing Exceptional Service

In the yoga instruction business, delivering exceptional service is paramount. It's not just about teaching poses; it's about nurturing strong connections with your students and fostering a warm, supportive community. By adopting a student-centric approach, creating an inviting class atmosphere, and offering personalized guidance, adjustments, and modifications, you can make each student feel valued and supported on their yoga journey. Let's dive deeper into how you can achieve this.

Develop a Student-Centric Approach

Providing exceptional service starts with putting your students at the heart of everything you do. This means understanding and supporting each individual's unique yoga journey. Here's how you can do it:

1. **Listen Actively**: Make it a priority to listen to your students' goals, challenges, and feedback. When you actively listen, you can tailor your instruction to meet their specific needs, making them feel heard and understood.
2. **Assess Student Abilities**: Take the time to observe and assess your students' levels of yoga experience, physical limitations, and

individual goals. This will help you provide appropriate modifications and variations during class to suit their needs.

3. **Offer Individualized Attention**: During your classes, strive to give personalized attention to each student. Offer feedback, guidance, and adjustments to help them deepen their practice and ensure proper alignment.

4. **Create a Supportive Environment**: Foster an atmosphere where students feel safe and comfortable to explore their practice. Encourage questions, provide positive reinforcement, and maintain a non-judgmental space.

Create a Welcoming and Inclusive Class Environment

To truly provide exceptional service, your class environment needs to be welcoming and inclusive. Here's how you can create such a space:

1. **Develop a Warm and Inviting Space**: Ensure your studio is clean, aesthetically pleasing, and well-ventilated to promote relaxation and tranquility.

2. **Set Clear Expectations**: Establish a class culture that promotes respect, acceptance, and inclusivity. Clearly communicate class guidelines and expectations so all students feel comfortable and valued.

3. **Encourage Self-Reflection**: Incorporate moments of self-reflection and mindfulness

into your classes. Guide students to connect with their body, breath, and emotions during their practice.

4. **Cultivate Community**: Create opportunities for students to connect outside of class through social events, workshops, or retreats. Fostering a sense of belonging can enhance their overall yoga experience.

Provide Personalized Guidance, Adjustments, and Modifications

Each student brings their unique needs and limitations to their yoga practice. Offering personalized guidance, adjustments, and modifications ensures they can practice safely and effectively. Here's how you can do this:

1. **Tailor Instruction to Individual Abilities:** Adapt your teaching style and language to cater to the diverse needs of your students. Offer modifications and variations for different skill levels and physical capabilities.
2. **Encourage Open Communication:** Create an environment where students feel comfortable expressing their concerns, limitations, and preferences. Regularly check in with them and encourage open communication about any discomfort or specific needs.
3. **Provide Hands-On Adjustments:** Offer gentle and appropriate hands-on adjustments to help students improve alignment, deepen stretches, and avoid

injury. Always seek consent and be mindful of personal boundaries.

4. **Offer Modifications and Alternatives:** Recognize that students may have physical limitations or injuries. Provide modifications and alternatives for poses to ensure everyone can participate fully without feeling excluded.

5. **Continuously Educate Yourself:** Stay up-to-date with the latest research and industry trends. Attend workshops, conferences, and seminars to expand your knowledge and enhance your teaching skills. This ongoing education allows you to better serve your students.

By embracing a student-centric approach, creating a welcoming and inclusive class environment, and offering personalized guidance, you can provide exceptional service in your yoga instruction business. Remember, in yoga, the journey is just as important as the destination. Your role as an instructor is to guide and support your students every step of the way.

Chapter 10: Growing Your Yoga Instruction Business

Hey there, yoga entrepreneur! You've laid the foundation for your yoga instruction business, and now it's time to focus on growth. Growing your yoga instruction business involves strategies to retain existing students, generate referrals, and continually expand and evolve your offerings. By focusing on exceptional teaching, staying connected with your community, and investing in your professional development, you can foster growth and success in your business. Let's dive in!

Retaining Existing Students

Keeping your current students happy and engaged is crucial for the long-term success of your yoga instruction business. By providing exceptional teaching and delivering results, you'll create a positive experience that keeps students coming back. Here are some strategies to help you retain your students:

1. **Consistency:** Maintain a consistent class schedule so students can rely on regular classes. Consistency should also apply to the quality of your teaching and the atmosphere of your classes.
2. **Personalization:** Get to know your students individually and understand their

goals, challenges, and preferences. Tailor your instruction to meet their specific needs, providing personalized guidance and modifications.

3. **Progress Tracking:** Help your students track their progress by offering periodic assessments, goal-setting sessions, or progress journals. Celebrate their achievements and provide encouragement and support throughout their yoga journey.

4. **Community Building:** Foster a sense of community within your classes by creating opportunities for students to connect and support one another. Encourage group activities or organize yoga retreats and social events to strengthen the bond among your students.

5. **Communication:** Establish open lines of communication with your students. Encourage them to provide feedback, ask questions, and share their experiences. Actively listen to their suggestions and make adjustments to improve their experience.

Generating Referrals

Referrals are a powerful source of new clients for your yoga instruction business. When your current students have positive experiences and see the value of your teaching, they're likely to recommend your classes to their friends, family, and colleagues. Here are some strategies to generate referrals:

1. **Incentives:** Offer incentives for referrals, such as discounted class packages, free

workshops, or special promotions. Encourage your students to spread the word about your classes and reward them for their support.

2. **Referral Programs:** Implement a formal referral program that rewards students for each new client they bring in. Provide clear guidelines and incentives to motivate your students to actively refer others to your classes.

3. **Testimonials:** Ask satisfied students to provide testimonials about their experience with your yoga instruction. Display these testimonials on your website, social media platforms, or promotional materials to build trust and credibility with potential clients.

4. **Partner with Local Businesses:** Collaborate with local businesses, such as wellness centers, fitness studios, or healthy cafes, to cross-promote your services. Offer joint promotions or referral discounts to encourage their clients to try your classes.

Expanding Class Offerings and Target Market Segments

As your yoga instruction business grows, it's important to continually assess and expand your class offerings and target market segments to meet the evolving needs and demands of your students. Here are some strategies to consider:

1. **Diversify Class Formats:** Offer a variety of class formats to cater to different preferences and fitness levels. Consider

adding formats such as hot yoga, prenatal yoga, meditation classes, or specialized workshops.

2. **Target Special Populations:** Identify niche markets or specific populations that could benefit from yoga instruction. This could include seniors, pregnant women, individuals with specific health conditions, or athletes. Customize your classes and marketing approach to address their unique needs and goals.

3. **Collaborate with Other Instructors:** Partner with other yoga instructors or fitness professionals to expand your class offerings. Consider co-teaching workshops, hosting guest instructors, or organizing events that showcase different teaching styles and expertise.

4. **Incorporate Online Classes:** Expand your reach by offering online classes or creating digital content such as guided meditations, posture tutorials, or yoga challenges. This allows you to reach a wider audience and supplement your in-person classes.

Continual Professional Development and Community Connection

Investing in your professional development is crucial to staying current, deepening your knowledge, and providing the best possible yoga instruction. Continually learning and expanding your expertise will also help you stay connected with your yoga community. Consider the following strategies:

1. **Attend Workshops and Trainings:** Participate in workshops, seminars, and advanced trainings to enhance your teaching skills, explore different yoga styles, and deepen your knowledge of yoga philosophy and anatomy.

2. **Join Professional Associations:** Join professional associations, such as Yoga Alliance, to gain access to resources, networking opportunities, and recognition within the yoga community. Engage with other yoga instructors to share ideas and learn from their experiences.

3. **Continuing Education:** Commit to ongoing self-study and research to keep up with emerging trends and developments in the field of yoga. Stay informed about the latest research, teaching methodologies, and advancements in yoga practice.

4. **Engage with Your Community:** Stay connected with your yoga community by attending local events, participating in yoga challenges or workshops, or hosting meet-ups. Collaborate with other yoga instructors, wellness practitioners, or local businesses to build a strong network and support system.

By implementing these strategies, you can foster growth in your yoga instruction business, continue to provide exceptional teaching, and make a positive impact on your students' lives. Stay committed to your own growth as a yoga instructor, and your business will thrive. Namaste!

www.ingramcontent.com/pod-product-compliance
Lightning Source LLC
Chambersburg PA
CBHW070138230526
45472CB00004B/1592